SMOKY

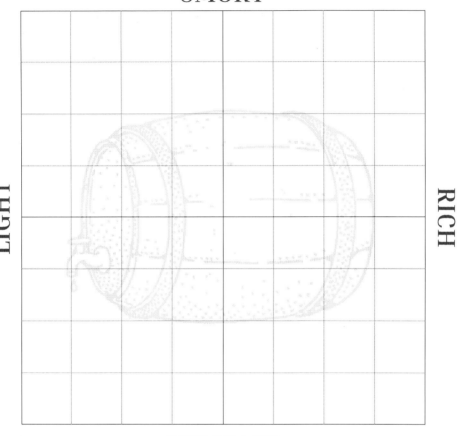

LIGHT

RICH

DELICATE

WHISKEYS

4	29	
5	30	
6	31	
7	32	
8	33	
9	34	
10	35	
11	36	
12	37	
13	38	
14	39	
15	40	
16	41	
17	42	
18	43	
19	44	
20	45	
21	46	
22	47	
23	48	
24	49	
25	50	
26	51	
27	52	
28	53	

WHISKEYS

WHISKEY

Old Putney

Distiller

Origin

Location **Work**

Date **5/20/23**

Strength

Price

TASTE

Delicate |—+—X—+—+—+—+—+—+—| Smoky

Light |—+—+—+—+—+—+—X—+—| Rich

GLANCE

Oily

Watery

COLOR

- Dark oak
- Mahogany
- Copper
- Amber
- Gold
- Honey
- Straw
- White wine
- Clear

WHEEL OF FLAVORS

Sweet
Honey
Fruity
Nutty
Floral
Malty
Body
Spicy
Smoky
Winey
Tobacco
Medicinal

OBSERVATIONS

4

WHISKEY
Dalmore

Distiller

Date 3/20/23

Origin

Strength

Location Highland

Price 69⁰⁰

TASTE

Delicate ├──┼──┼──Ø──┼──┼──┤ Smoky

Light ├──┼──┼──Ø──┼──┼──┤ Rich

GLANCE

Oily

Watery

COLOR

Dark oak

Mahogany

Copper

(Amber)

Gold

Honey

Straw

White wine

Clear

WHEEL OF FLAVORS

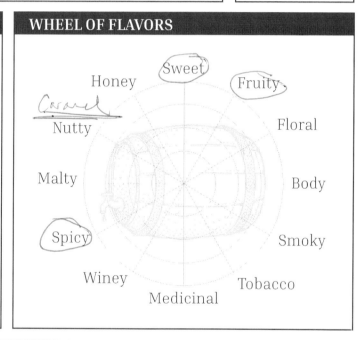

Honey · (Sweet) · (Fruity)

Caramel

Nutty · Floral

Malty · Body

(Spicy) · Smoky

Winey · Tobacco

Medicinal

OBSERVATIONS

WHISKEY

Macallan 12

Distiller

Origin

Location Speyside

Date 5/20/25

Strength

Price

TASTE

Delicate |—+—+—+—+—+—+—+—| Smoky

Light |—+—+—+—+—+—+—+—| Rich

GLANCE

Oily

Watery

COLOR

Dark oak

Mahogany

Copper

Amber

Gold

Honey

Straw

White wine

Clear

WHEEL OF FLAVORS

Sweet
Honey   Fruity
Nutty   Floral
Malty   Body
Spicy   Smoky
Winey   Tobacco
Medicinal

OBSERVATIONS

WHISKEY

Auchentoshan

RATING

Distiller

Origin

Location Lowland

Date

Strength

Price $45

TASTE

Delicate |———|———|———|———|———|———|———| Smoky

Light |———|———|———|———|———|———|———| Rich

GLANCE

Oily

(Watery)

COLOR

- Dark oak
- Mahogany
- Copper
- Amber
- Gold
- Honey
- (Straw)
- White wine
- Clear

WHEEL OF FLAVORS

Sweet

Honey   Fruity

Nutty   Floral

(Malty)   Body

Spicy   (Smoky)

Winey   Tobacco

Medicinal

OBSERVATIONS

triple distilled
40

WHISKEY LAGAVULLN

RATING

Distiller _____   Date _____

Origin _____ _lleyn_____   Strength _____

Location _____   Price _____

TASTE

Delicate ├──┼──┼──┼──┼──┼──┼──┤ Smoky

Light ├──┼──┼──┼──┼──┼──┼──┤ Rich

GLANCE

Oily

Watery

COLOR

Dark oak

Mahogany

(Copper)

Amber

Gold

Honey

Straw

White wine

Clear

WHEEL OF FLAVORS

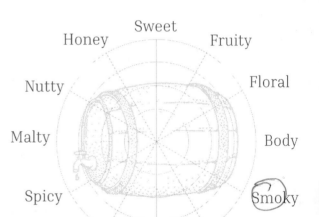

Sweet

Honey   Fruity

Nutty   Floral

Malty   Body

Spicy   (Smoky)

Winey   (Tobacco)

Medicinal

OBSERVATIONS

WHISKEY

Distiller _____ Date _____

Origin _____ Strength _____

Location _____ Price _____

TASTE

Delicate ├──┼──┼──┼──┼──┼──┤ Smoky

Light ├──┼──┼──┼──┼──┼──┤ Rich

GLANCE

Oily

Watery

COLOR

Dark oak

Mahogany

Copper

Amber

Gold

Honey

Straw

White wine

Clear

WHEEL OF FLAVORS

Sweet

Honey

Fruity

Nutty

Floral

Malty

Body

Spicy

Smoky

Winey

Tobacco

Medicinal

OBSERVATIONS

WHISKEY

RATING

Distiller _____   Date _____

Origin _____   Strength _____

Location _____   Price _____

TASTE

Delicate ├──┼──┼──┼──┼──┼──┼──┤ Smoky

Light ├──┼──┼──┼──┼──┼──┼──┤ Rich

GLANCE

Oily

Watery

COLOR

Dark oak

Mahogany

Copper

Amber

Gold

Honey

Straw

White wine

Clear

WHEEL OF FLAVORS

Sweet

Honey   Fruity

Nutty   Floral

Malty   Body

Spicy   Smoky

Winey   Tobacco

Medicinal

OBSERVATIONS

WHISKEY

RATING

Distiller

Date

Origin

Strength

Location

Price

TASTE

Delicate |—|—|—|—|—|—|—| Smoky

Light |—|—|—|—|—|—|—| Rich

GLANCE

Oily

Watery

COLOR

Dark oak

Mahogany

Copper

Amber

Gold

Honey

Straw

White wine

Clear

WHEEL OF FLAVORS

Sweet

Honey   Fruity

Nutty   Floral

Malty   Body

Spicy   Smoky

Winey   Tobacco

Medicinal

OBSERVATIONS

WHISKEY

RATING

Distiller _____   Date _____

Origin _____   Strength _____

Location _____   Price _____

TASTE

Delicate |—+—+—+—+—|—+—+—+—+—| Smoky

Light |—+—+—+—+—|—+—+—+—+—| Rich

GLANCE

Oily

Watery

COLOR

- Dark oak
- Mahogany
- Copper
- Amber
- Gold
- Honey
- Straw
- White wine
- Clear

WHEEL OF FLAVORS

Sweet

Honey

Fruity

Nutty

Floral

Malty

Body

Spicy

Smoky

Winey

Tobacco

Medicinal

OBSERVATIONS

_____

_____

_____

_____

WHISKEY

RATING

Distiller   Date

Origin _____   Strength _____

Location _____   Price _____

TASTE

Delicate ├──┼──┼──┼──┼──┼──┤ Smoky

Light ├──┼──┼──┼──┼──┼──┤ Rich

GLANCE

Oily

Watery

COLOR

Dark oak

Mahogany

Copper

Amber

Gold

Honey

Straw

White wine

Clear

WHEEL OF FLAVORS

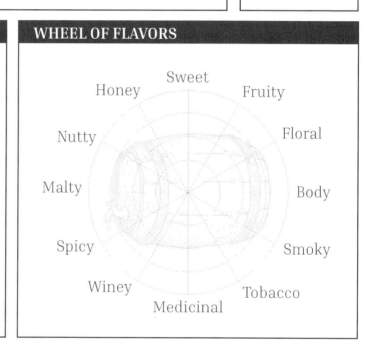

Sweet

Honey

Fruity

Nutty

Floral

Malty

Body

Spicy

Smoky

Winey

Tobacco

Medicinal

OBSERVATIONS

_____
_____
_____

WHISKEY

Distiller _____ Date _____

Origin _____ Strength _____

Location _____ Price _____

TASTE

Delicate ├──┼──┼──┼──┼──┼──┼──┤ Smoky

Light ├──┼──┼──┼──┼──┼──┼──┤ Rich

GLANCE

Oily

Watery

COLOR

Dark oak

Mahogany

Copper

Amber

Gold

Honey

Straw

White wine

Clear

WHEEL OF FLAVORS

Sweet

Honey

Fruity

Nutty

Floral

Malty

Body

Spicy

Smoky

Winey

Tobacco

Medicinal

OBSERVATIONS

WHISKEY

Distiller   Date

Origin   Strength

Location   Price

TASTE

Delicate |——+——+——+——|——+——+——+——| Smoky

Light |——+——+——+——|——+——+——+——| Rich

GLANCE

Oily

Watery

COLOR

Dark oak

Mahogany

Copper

Amber

Gold

Honey

Straw

White wine

Clear

WHEEL OF FLAVORS

Sweet

Honey   Fruity

Nutty   Floral

Malty   Body

Spicy   Smoky

Winey   Tobacco

Medicinal

OBSERVATIONS

WHISKEY

RATING

Distiller

Origin

Location

Date

Strength

Price

TASTE

Delicate ├──┼──┼──┼──┼──┼──┼──┤ Smoky

Light ├──┼──┼──┼──┼──┼──┼──┤ Rich

GLANCE

Oily

Watery

COLOR

Dark oak

Mahogany

Copper

Amber

Gold

Honey

Straw

White wine

Clear

WHEEL OF FLAVORS

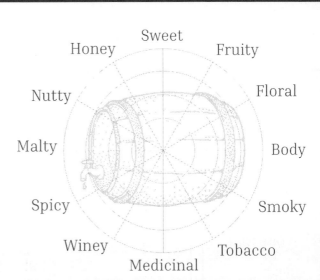

Sweet

Honey

Fruity

Nutty

Floral

Malty

Body

Spicy

Smoky

Winey

Tobacco

Medicinal

OBSERVATIONS

WHISKEY

Distiller

Origin

Location

Date

Strength

Price

TASTE

Delicate |——|——|——|——|——|——| Smoky

Light |——|——|——|——|——|——| Rich

GLANCE

Oily

Watery

COLOR

Dark oak

Mahogany

Copper

Amber

Gold

Honey

Straw

White wine

Clear

WHEEL OF FLAVORS

Sweet

Honey

Fruity

Nutty

Floral

Malty

Body

Spicy

Smoky

Winey

Tobacco

Medicinal

OBSERVATIONS

WHISKEY

Distiller

Origin

Location

Date

Strength

Price

TASTE

Delicate ├──┼──┼──┼──┼──┼──┼──┤ Smoky

Light ├──┼──┼──┼──┼──┼──┼──┤ Rich

GLANCE

Oily

Watery

COLOR

Dark oak

Mahogany

Copper

Amber

Gold

Honey

Straw

White wine

Clear

WHEEL OF FLAVORS

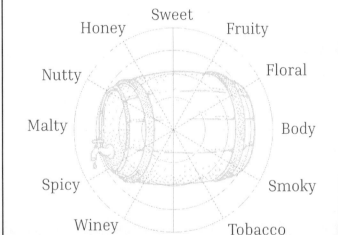

Sweet

Honey

Fruity

Nutty

Floral

Malty

Body

Spicy

Smoky

Winey

Tobacco

Medicinal

OBSERVATIONS

WHISKEY

RATING

Distiller

Origin

Location

Date

Strength

Price

TASTE

Delicate ├──┼──┼──┼──┼──┼──┼──┤ Smoky

Light ├──┼──┼──┼──┼──┼──┼──┤ Rich

GLANCE

Oily

Watery

COLOR

Dark oak

Mahogany

Copper

Amber

Gold

Honey

Straw

White wine

Clear

WHEEL OF FLAVORS

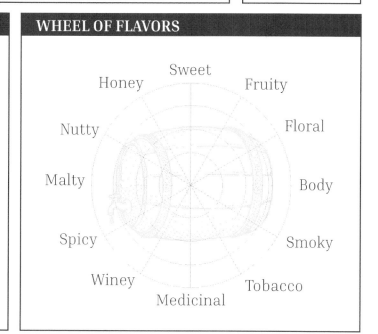

Sweet

Honey   Fruity

Nutty   Floral

Malty   Body

Spicy   Smoky

Winey   Tobacco

Medicinal

OBSERVATIONS

WHISKEY

Distiller

Origin

Location

Date

Strength

Price

TASTE

Delicate |———+———+———+———|———+———+———+———| Smoky

Light |———+———+———+———|———+———+———+———| Rich

GLANCE

Oily

Watery

COLOR

Dark oak

Mahogany

Copper

Amber

Gold

Honey

Straw

White wine

Clear

WHEEL OF FLAVORS

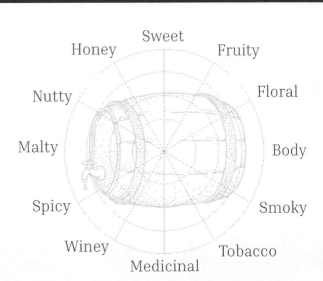

Sweet

Honey

Fruity

Nutty

Floral

Malty

Body

Spicy

Smoky

Winey

Tobacco

Medicinal

OBSERVATIONS

WHISKEY

RATING

Distiller

Date

Origin

Strength

Location

Price

TASTE

Delicate |—————| Smoky

Light |—————| Rich

GLANCE

Oily

Watery

COLOR

Dark oak

Mahogany

Copper

Amber

Gold

Honey

Straw

White wine

Clear

WHEEL OF FLAVORS

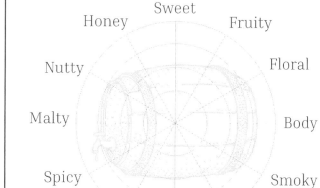

Sweet

Honey   Fruity

Nutty   Floral

Malty   Body

Spicy   Smoky

Winey   Tobacco

Medicinal

OBSERVATIONS

WHISKEY

Distiller _____   Date _____

Origin _____   Strength _____

Location _____   Price _____

TASTE

Delicate |—+—+—+—+—+—+—+—+—| Smoky

Light |—+—+—+—+—+—+—+—+—| Rich

GLANCE

Oily

Watery

COLOR

Dark oak

Mahogany

Copper

Amber

Gold

Honey

Straw

White wine

Clear

WHEEL OF FLAVORS

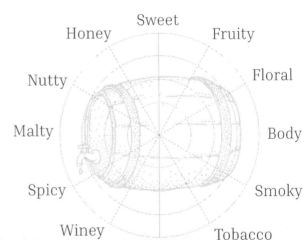

Sweet

Honey   Fruity

Nutty   Floral

Malty   Body

Spicy   Smoky

Winey   Tobacco

Medicinal

OBSERVATIONS

WHISKEY

RATING

Distiller

Origin

Location

Date

Strength

Price

TASTE

Delicate |—+—+—+—|—+—+—+—| Smoky

Light |—+—+—+—|—+—+—+—| Rich

GLANCE

Oily

Watery

COLOR

Dark oak

Mahogany

Copper

Amber

Gold

Honey

Straw

White wine

Clear

WHEEL OF FLAVORS

Sweet

Honey

Fruity

Nutty

Floral

Malty

Body

Spicy

Smoky

Winey

Tobacco

Medicinal

OBSERVATIONS

WHISKEY

RATING

Distiller ....

Origin ....

Location ....

Date ....

Strength ....

Price ....

TASTE

Delicate ├──┼──┼──┼──┼──┼──┼──┤ Smoky

Light ├──┼──┼──┼──┼──┼──┼──┤ Rich

GLANCE

Oily

Watery

COLOR

Dark oak

Mahogany

Copper

Amber

Gold

Honey

Straw

White wine

Clear

WHEEL OF FLAVORS

Sweet

Honey

Fruity

Nutty

Floral

Malty

Body

Spicy

Smoky

Winey

Tobacco

Medicinal

OBSERVATIONS

WHISKEY

RATING

Distiller _____ Date _____

Origin _____ Strength _____

Location _____ Price _____

TASTE

Delicate |—+—+—+—+—+—+—| Smoky

Light |—+—+—+—+—+—+—| Rich

GLANCE

 Oily

Watery

COLOR

Dark oak

Mahogany

Copper

Amber

Gold

Honey

Straw

White wine

Clear

WHEEL OF FLAVORS

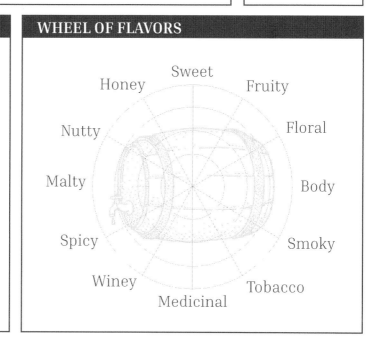

Sweet

Honey

Fruity

Nutty

Floral

Malty

Body

Spicy

Smoky

Winey

Tobacco

Medicinal

OBSERVATIONS

WHISKEY

RATING

Distiller		Date	
Origin		Strength	
Location		Price	

TASTE

Delicate ├─┼─┼─┼─┼─┼─┼─┤ Smoky

Light ├─┼─┼─┼─┼─┼─┼─┤ Rich

GLANCE

Oily

Watery

COLOR

Dark oak
Mahogany
Copper
Amber
Gold
Honey
Straw
White wine
Clear

WHEEL OF FLAVORS

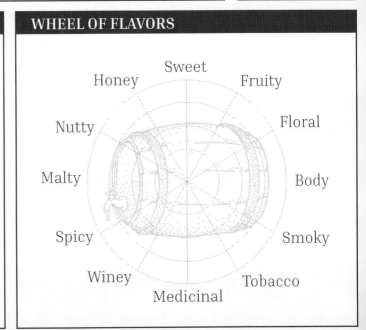

Sweet
Honey
Fruity
Nutty
Floral
Malty
Body
Spicy
Smoky
Winey
Tobacco
Medicinal

OBSERVATIONS

WHISKEY

RATING

Distiller

Origin

Location

Date

Strength

Price

TASTE

Delicate ├──┼──┼──┼──┼──┼──┼──┤ Smoky

Light ├──┼──┼──┼──┼──┼──┼──┤ Rich

GLANCE

Oily

Watery

COLOR

Dark oak

Mahogany

Copper

Amber

Gold

Honey

Straw

White wine

Clear

WHEEL OF FLAVORS

Sweet

Honey

Fruity

Nutty

Floral

Malty

Body

Spicy

Smoky

Winey

Tobacco

Medicinal

OBSERVATIONS

WHISKEY

RATING

Distiller _____   Date _____

Origin _____   Strength _____

Location _____   Price _____

TASTE

Delicate |—+—+—+—+—+—+—+—| Smoky

Light |—+—+—+—+—+—+—+—| Rich

GLANCE

Oily

Watery

COLOR

Dark oak

Mahogany

Copper

Amber

Gold

Honey

Straw

White wine

Clear

WHEEL OF FLAVORS

Sweet

Honey

Fruity

Nutty

Floral

Malty

Body

Spicy

Smoky

Winey

Tobacco

Medicinal

OBSERVATIONS

WHISKEY

Distiller

Date

Origin

Strength

Location

Price

TASTE

Delicate |———+———+———+———+———| Smoky

Light |———+———+———+———+———| Rich

GLANCE

Oily

Watery

COLOR

Dark oak

Mahogany

Copper

Amber

Gold

Honey

Straw

White wine

Clear

WHEEL OF FLAVORS

Sweet

Honey

Fruity

Nutty

Floral

Malty

Body

Spicy

Smoky

Winey

Tobacco

Medicinal

OBSERVATIONS

WHISKEY

RATING

Distiller

Origin

Location

Date

Strength

Price

TASTE

Delicate |—|—|—|—|—|—|—|—| Smoky

Light |—|—|—|—|—|—|—|—| Rich

GLANCE

Oily

Watery

COLOR

Dark oak

Mahogany

Copper

Amber

Gold

Honey

Straw

White wine

Clear

WHEEL OF FLAVORS

Sweet

Honey   Fruity

Nutty   Floral

Malty   Body

Spicy   Smoky

Winey   Tobacco

Medicinal

OBSERVATIONS

WHISKEY

Distiller _____ Date _____

Origin _____ Strength _____

Location _____ Price _____

TASTE

Delicate ├──┼──┼──┼──┼──┼──┼──┤ Smoky

Light ├──┼──┼──┼──┼──┼──┼──┤ Rich

GLANCE

Oily

Watery

COLOR

Dark oak

Mahogany

Copper

Amber

Gold

Honey

Straw

White wine

Clear

WHEEL OF FLAVORS

Sweet

Honey

Fruity

Nutty

Floral

Malty

Body

Spicy

Smoky

Winey

Tobacco

Medicinal

OBSERVATIONS

WHISKEY

Distiller

Origin

Location

Date

Strength

Price

TASTE

Delicate ├──┼──┼──┼──┼──┼──┼──┤ Smoky

Light ├──┼──┼──┼──┼──┼──┼──┤ Rich

GLANCE

Oily

Watery

COLOR

Dark oak

Mahogany

Copper

Amber

Gold

Honey

Straw

White wine

Clear

WHEEL OF FLAVORS

Sweet

Honey   Fruity

Nutty   Floral

Malty   Body

Spicy   Smoky

Winey   Tobacco

Medicinal

OBSERVATIONS

WHISKEY

RATING

Distiller   Date

Origin   Strength

Location   Price

TASTE

Delicate ├──┼──┼──┼──┼──┼──┼──┤ Smoky

Light ├──┼──┼──┼──┼──┼──┼──┤ Rich

GLANCE

Oily

Watery

COLOR

Dark oak

Mahogany

Copper

Amber

Gold

Honey

Straw

White wine

Clear

WHEEL OF FLAVORS

Sweet

Honey   Fruity

Nutty   Floral

Malty   Body

Spicy   Smoky

Winey   Tobacco

Medicinal

OBSERVATIONS

WHISKEY

Distiller ....

Origin ....

Location ....

Date ....

Strength ....

Price ....

TASTE

Delicate |—+—+—+—+—|—+—+—+—+—| Smoky

Light |—+—+—+—|—+—+—+—| Rich

GLANCE

Oily

Watery

COLOR

Dark oak

Mahogany

Copper

Amber

Gold

Honey

Straw

White wine

Clear

WHEEL OF FLAVORS

Sweet

Honey   Fruity

Nutty   Floral

Malty   Body

Spicy   Smoky

Winey   Tobacco

Medicinal

OBSERVATIONS

WHISKEY

Distiller

Origin

Location

Date

Strength

Price

TASTE

Delicate |———————————| Smoky

Light |———————————| Rich

GLANCE

Oily

Watery

COLOR

- Dark oak
- Mahogany
- Copper
- Amber
- Gold
- Honey
- Straw
- White wine
- Clear

WHEEL OF FLAVORS

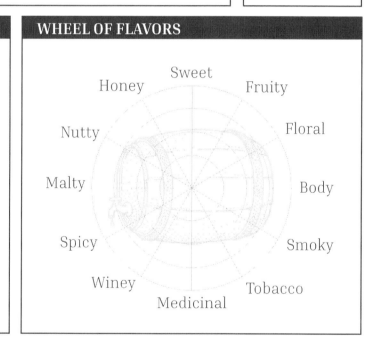

Sweet

Honey   Fruity

Nutty   Floral

Malty   Body

Spicy   Smoky

Winey   Tobacco

Medicinal

OBSERVATIONS

WHISKEY

RATING

Distiller _____ Date _____

Origin _____ Strength _____

Location _____ Price _____

TASTE

Delicate ├──┼──┼──┼──┼──┼──┼──┤ Smoky

Light ├──┼──┼──┼──┼──┼──┼──┤ Rich

GLANCE

Oily

Watery

COLOR

Dark oak

Mahogany

Copper

Amber

Gold

Honey

Straw

White wine

Clear

WHEEL OF FLAVORS

Sweet

Honey

Fruity

Nutty

Floral

Malty

Body

Spicy

Smoky

Winey

Tobacco

Medicinal

OBSERVATIONS

WHISKEY

	RATING

Distiller   Date

Origin _____   Strength _____

Location _____   Price _____

TASTE

Delicate |—+—+—+—+—+—+—+—| Smoky

Light |—+—+—+—+—+—+—+—| Rich

GLANCE

Oily

Watery

COLOR

Dark oak

Mahogany

Copper

Amber

Gold

Honey

Straw

White wine

Clear

WHEEL OF FLAVORS

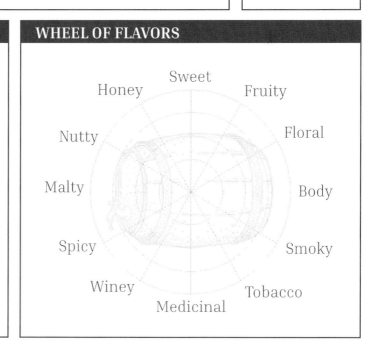

Sweet
Honey
Fruity
Nutty
Floral
Malty
Body
Spicy
Smoky
Winey
Tobacco
Medicinal

OBSERVATIONS

WHISKEY

RATING

Distiller ....

Origin ....

Location ....

Date ....

Strength ....

Price ....

TASTE

Delicate ├──┼──┼──┼──┼──┼──┼──┤ Smoky

Light ├──┼──┼──┼──┼──┼──┼──┤ Rich

GLANCE

Oily

Watery

COLOR

Dark oak

Mahogany

Copper

Amber

Gold

Honey

Straw

White wine

Clear

WHEEL OF FLAVORS

Sweet

Honey

Fruity

Nutty

Floral

Malty

Body

Spicy

Smoky

Winey

Tobacco

Medicinal

OBSERVATIONS

....

....

....

....

WHISKEY

RATING

Distiller   Date

Origin ....   Strength ....

Location ....   Price ....

TASTE

Delicate ├──┼──┼──┼──┼──┼──┼──┤ Smoky

Light ├──┼──┼──┼──┼──┼──┼──┤ Rich

GLANCE

Oily

Watery

COLOR

Dark oak

Mahogany

Copper

Amber

Gold

Honey

Straw

White wine

Clear

WHEEL OF FLAVORS

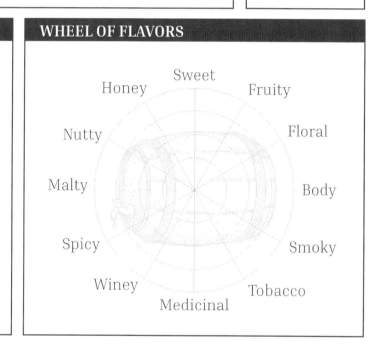

Sweet

Honey   Fruity

Nutty   Floral

Malty   Body

Spicy   Smoky

Winey   Tobacco

Medicinal

OBSERVATIONS

WHISKEY

Distiller ....

Date ....

Origin ....

Strength ....

Location ....

Price ....

TASTE

Delicate ├──┼──┼──┼──┼──┼──┼──┤ Smoky

Light ├──┼──┼──┼──┼──┼──┼──┤ Rich

GLANCE

Oily

Watery

COLOR

Dark oak

Mahogany

Copper

Amber

Gold

Honey

Straw

White wine

Clear

WHEEL OF FLAVORS

Sweet

Honey   Fruity

Nutty   Floral

Malty   Body

Spicy   Smoky

Winey   Tobacco

Medicinal

OBSERVATIONS

WHISKEY

Distiller

Origin

Location

Date

Strength

Price

TASTE

Delicate |————————| Smoky

Light |————————| Rich

GLANCE

Oily

Watery

COLOR

Dark oak

Mahogany

Copper

Amber

Gold

Honey

Straw

White wine

Clear

WHEEL OF FLAVORS

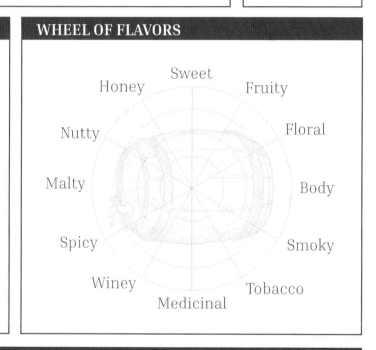

Sweet

Honey   Fruity

Nutty   Floral

Malty   Body

Spicy   Smoky

Winey   Tobacco

Medicinal

OBSERVATIONS

WHISKEY

Distiller

Origin

Location

Date

Strength

Price

TASTE

Delicate ├──┼──┼──┼──┼──┼──┼──┼──┤ Smoky

Light ├──┼──┼──┼──┼──┼──┼──┼──┤ Rich

GLANCE

Oily

Watery

COLOR

Dark oak

Mahogany

Copper

Amber

Gold

Honey

Straw

White wine

Clear

WHEEL OF FLAVORS

Sweet

Honey

Fruity

Nutty

Floral

Malty

Body

Spicy

Smoky

Winey

Tobacco

Medicinal

OBSERVATIONS

WHISKEY

Distiller   Date

Origin   Strength

Location   Price

TASTE

Delicate |——+——+——+——+——+——+——| Smoky

Light |——+——+——+——+——+——+——| Rich

GLANCE

Oily

Watery

COLOR

Dark oak

Mahogany

Copper

Amber

Gold

Honey

Straw

White wine

Clear

WHEEL OF FLAVORS

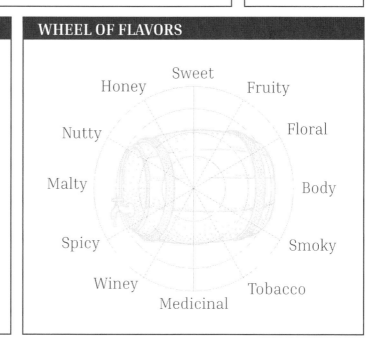

Sweet

Honey   Fruity

Nutty   Floral

Malty   Body

Spicy   Smoky

Winey   Tobacco

Medicinal

OBSERVATIONS

WHISKEY

Distiller .... Date ....

Origin .... Strength ....

Location .... Price ....

TASTE

Delicate ├──┼──┼──┼──┼──┼──┼──┤ Smoky

Light ├──┼──┼──┼──┼──┼──┼──┤ Rich

GLANCE

Oily

Watery

COLOR

Dark oak

Mahogany

Copper

Amber

Gold

Honey

Straw

White wine

Clear

WHEEL OF FLAVORS

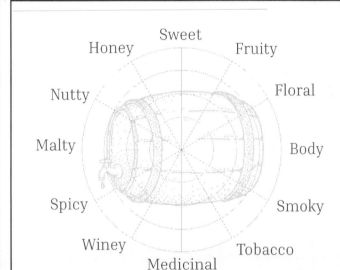

Sweet

Honey

Fruity

Nutty

Floral

Malty

Body

Spicy

Smoky

Winey

Tobacco

Medicinal

OBSERVATIONS

WHISKEY

RATING

Distiller   Date

Origin   Strength

Location   Price

TASTE

Delicate |———|———|———|———|———|———|———| Smoky

Light |———|———|———|———|———|———|———| Rich

GLANCE

Oily

Watery

COLOR

Dark oak

Mahogany

Copper

Amber

Gold

Honey

Straw

White wine

Clear

WHEEL OF FLAVORS

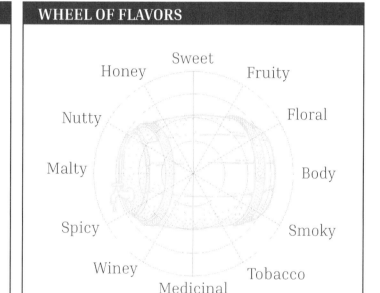

Sweet

Honey   Fruity

Nutty   Floral

Malty   Body

Spicy   Smoky

Winey   Tobacco

Medicinal

OBSERVATIONS

WHISKEY

Distiller _____   Date _____

Origin _____   Strength _____

Location _____   Price _____

TASTE

Delicate ├──┼──┼──┼──┼──┼──┼──┤ Smoky

Light ├──┼──┼──┼──┼──┼──┼──┤ Rich

GLANCE

Oily

Watery

COLOR

Dark oak

Mahogany

Copper

Amber

Gold

Honey

Straw

White wine

Clear

WHEEL OF FLAVORS

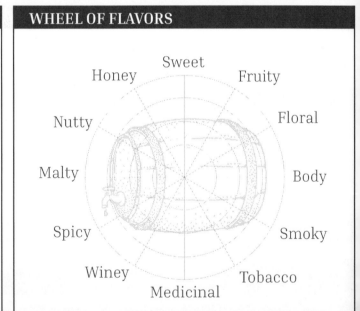

Sweet

Honey

Fruity

Nutty

Floral

Malty

Body

Spicy

Smoky

Winey

Tobacco

Medicinal

OBSERVATIONS

WHISKEY

| | RATING |

Distiller   **Date**

Origin   **Strength**

Location   **Price**

TASTE

Delicate |———+———+———+———+———+———| Smoky

Light |———+———+———+———+———+———| Rich

GLANCE

Oily

Watery

COLOR

Dark oak

Mahogany

Copper

Amber

Gold

Honey

Straw

White wine

Clear

WHEEL OF FLAVORS

Sweet

Honey

Fruity

Nutty

Floral

Malty

Body

Spicy

Smoky

Winey

Tobacco

Medicinal

OBSERVATIONS

WHISKEY

Distiller

Origin

Location

Date

Strength

Price

TASTE

Delicate ├──┼──┼──┼──┼──┼──┼──┤ Smoky

Light ├──┼──┼──┼──┼──┼──┼──┤ Rich

GLANCE

Oily

Watery

COLOR

Dark oak

Mahogany

Copper

Amber

Gold

Honey

Straw

White wine

Clear

WHEEL OF FLAVORS

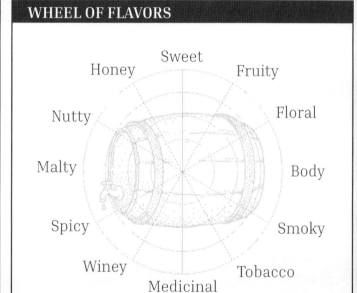

Sweet

Honey   Fruity

Nutty   Floral

Malty   Body

Spicy   Smoky

Winey   Tobacco

Medicinal

OBSERVATIONS

WHISKEY

RATING

Distiller   Date

Origin   Strength

Location   Price

TASTE

Delicate |———|———|———|———|———|———|———| Smoky

Light |———|———|———|———|———|———|———| Rich

GLANCE

Oily

Watery

COLOR

Dark oak

Mahogany

Copper

Amber

Gold

Honey

Straw

White wine

Clear

WHEEL OF FLAVORS

Sweet

Honey   Fruity

Nutty   Floral

Malty   Body

Spicy   Smoky

Winey   Tobacco

Medicinal

OBSERVATIONS

WHISKEY

Distiller _____

Date _____

Origin _____

Strength _____

Location _____

Price _____

TASTE

Delicate |——+——+——+——+——+——+——+——| Smoky

Light |——+——+——+——+——+——+——+——| Rich

GLANCE

Oily

Watery

COLOR

Dark oak

Mahogany

Copper

Amber

Gold

Honey

Straw

White wine

Clear

WHEEL OF FLAVORS

Sweet

Honey

Fruity

Nutty

Floral

Malty

Body

Spicy

Smoky

Winey

Tobacco

Medicinal

OBSERVATIONS

WHISKEY

RATING

Distiller

Origin

Location

Date

Strength

Price

TASTE

Delicate ├────┼──┼──┼──┼──┼──┼──┼──┤ Smoky

Light ├──┼──┼──┼──┼──┼──┼──┤ Rich

GLANCE

Oily

Watery

COLOR

Dark oak

Mahogany

Copper

Amber

Gold

Honey

Straw

White wine

Clear

WHEEL OF FLAVORS

Sweet

Honey

Fruity

Nutty

Floral

Malty

Body

Spicy

Smoky

Winey

Tobacco

Medicinal

OBSERVATIONS

WHISKEY

RATING

Distiller .... Date ....

Origin .... Strength ....

Location .... Price ....

TASTE

Delicate ├──┼──┼──┼──┼──┼──┼──┤ Smoky

Light ├──┼──┼──┼──┼──┼──┼──┤ Rich

GLANCE

Oily

Watery

COLOR

Dark oak

Mahogany

Copper

Amber

Gold

Honey

Straw

White wine

Clear

WHEEL OF FLAVORS

Sweet

Honey   Fruity

Nutty   Floral

Malty   Body

Spicy   Smoky

Winey   Tobacco

Medicinal

OBSERVATIONS

WHISKEY

RATING

Distiller   Date

Origin   Strength

Location   Price

TASTE

Delicate ├─────┼─────┼─────┼─────┼─────┤ Smoky

Light ├─────┼─────┼─────┼─────┼─────┤ Rich

GLANCE

 Oily

Watery

COLOR

Dark oak

Mahogany

Copper

Amber

Gold

Honey

Straw

White wine

Clear

WHEEL OF FLAVORS

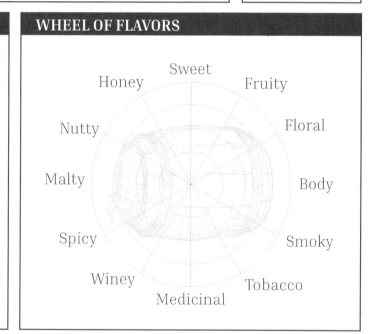

Sweet

Honey   Fruity

Nutty   Floral

Malty   Body

Spicy   Smoky

Winey   Tobacco

Medicinal

OBSERVATIONS

WHISKEY

Distiller _____ Date _____

Origin _____ Strength _____

Location _____ Price _____

TASTE

Delicate |—+—+—+—+—+—+—+—| Smoky

Light |—+—+—+—+—+—+—+—| Rich

GLANCE

Oily

Watery

COLOR

Dark oak

Mahogany

Copper

Amber

Gold

Honey

Straw

White wine

Clear

WHEEL OF FLAVORS

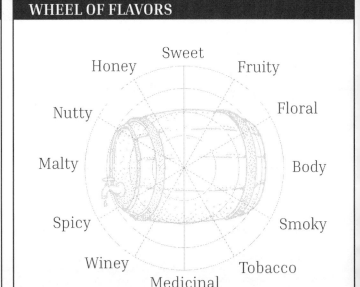

Sweet

Honey   Fruity

Nutty   Floral

Malty   Body

Spicy   Smoky

Winey   Tobacco

Medicinal

OBSERVATIONS

WHISKEY

RATING

Distiller

Date

Origin

Strength

Location

Price

TASTE

Delicate ├──┼──┼──┼──┼──┼──┤ Smoky

Light ├──┼──┼──┼──┼──┼──┤ Rich

GLANCE

Oily

Watery

COLOR

Dark oak

Mahogany

Copper

Amber

Gold

Honey

Straw

White wine

Clear

WHEEL OF FLAVORS

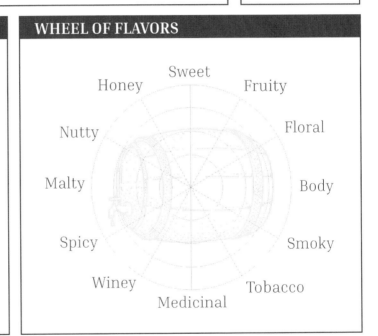

Sweet

Honey

Fruity

Nutty

Floral

Malty

Body

Spicy

Smoky

Winey

Tobacco

Medicinal

OBSERVATIONS

WHISKEY

Distiller _____ Date _____

Origin _____ Strength _____

Location _____ Price _____

TASTE

Delicate |—+——+——+——+——+——+——+——| Smoky

Light |—+——+——+——+——+——+——+——| Rich

GLANCE

Oily

Watery

COLOR

Dark oak
Mahogany
Copper
Amber
Gold
Honey
Straw
White wine
Clear

WHEEL OF FLAVORS

Sweet
Honey
Fruity
Nutty
Floral
Malty
Body
Spicy
Smoky
Winey
Tobacco
Medicinal

OBSERVATIONS

WHISKEY

Distiller   Date

Origin   Strength

Location   Price

TASTE

Delicate |——+——+——+——+——+——+——| Smoky

Light |——+——+——+——+——+——+——| Rich

GLANCE

Oily

Watery

COLOR

Dark oak

Mahogany

Copper

Amber

Gold

Honey

Straw

White wine

Clear

WHEEL OF FLAVORS

Sweet

Honey   Fruity

Nutty   Floral

Malty   Body

Spicy   Smoky

Winey   Tobacco

Medicinal

OBSERVATIONS

WHISKEY

RATING

Distiller ....
Origin ....
Location ....

Date ....
Strength ....
Price ....

TASTE

Delicate ├──┼──┼──┼──┼──┼──┼──┤ Smoky

Light ├──┼──┼──┼──┼──┼──┼──┤ Rich

GLANCE

Oily

Watery

COLOR

Dark oak
Mahogany
Copper
Amber
Gold
Honey
Straw
White wine
Clear

WHEEL OF FLAVORS

Sweet
Honey   Fruity
Nutty   Floral
Malty   Body
Spicy   Smoky
Winey   Tobacco
Medicinal

OBSERVATIONS

WHISKEY

RATING

Distiller

Origin

Location

Date

Strength

Price

TASTE

Delicate |—|—|—|—|—|—|—|—| Smoky

Light |—|—|—|—|—|—|—|—| Rich

GLANCE

Oily

Watery

COLOR

Dark oak

Mahogany

Copper

Amber

Gold

Honey

Straw

White wine

Clear

WHEEL OF FLAVORS

Sweet

Honey   Fruity

Nutty   Floral

Malty   Body

Spicy   Smoky

Winey   Tobacco

Medicinal

OBSERVATIONS

WHISKEY

Distiller ....

Origin ....

Location ....

Date ....

Strength ....

Price ....

TASTE

Delicate |—+—+—+—+—+—| Smoky

Light |—+—+—+—+—+—| Rich

GLANCE

Oily

Watery

COLOR

Dark oak

Mahogany

Copper

Amber

Gold

Honey

Straw

White wine

Clear

WHEEL OF FLAVORS

Sweet

Honey

Fruity

Nutty

Floral

Malty

Body

Spicy

Smoky

Winey

Tobacco

Medicinal

OBSERVATIONS

WHISKEY

Distiller   Date

Origin _____   Strength _____

Location _____   Price _____

TASTE

Delicate ├──┼──┼──┼──┼──┼──┤ Smoky

Light ├──┼──┼──┼──┼──┼──┤ Rich

GLANCE

Oily

Watery

COLOR

Dark oak

Mahogany

Copper

Amber

Gold

Honey

Straw

White wine

Clear

WHEEL OF FLAVORS

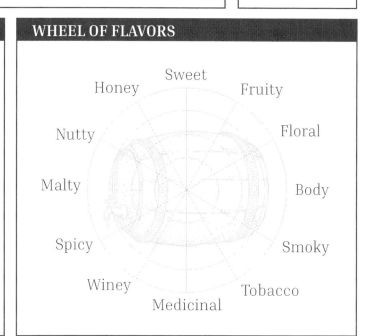

Sweet

Honey   Fruity

Nutty   Floral

Malty   Body

Spicy   Smoky

Winey   Tobacco

Medicinal

OBSERVATIONS

WHISKEY

Distiller _____ Date _____

Origin _____ Strength _____

Location _____ Price _____

TASTE

Delicate ├──┼──┼──┼──┼──┼──┼──┤ Smoky

Light ├──┼──┼──┼──┼──┼──┼──┤ Rich

GLANCE

Oily

Watery

COLOR

Dark oak

Mahogany

Copper

Amber

Gold

Honey

Straw

White wine

Clear

WHEEL OF FLAVORS

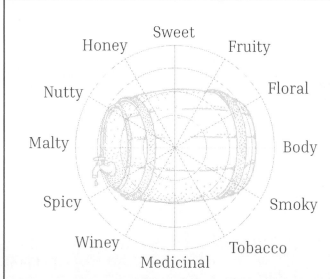

Sweet

Honey

Fruity

Nutty

Floral

Malty

Body

Spicy

Smoky

Winey

Tobacco

Medicinal

OBSERVATIONS

WHISKEY

Distiller

Date

Origin

Strength

Location

Price

TASTE

Delicate |———+———+———+———+———+———+———| Smoky

Light |———+———+———+———+———+———+———| Rich

GLANCE

Oily

Watery

COLOR

- Dark oak
- Mahogany
- Copper
- Amber
- Gold
- Honey
- Straw
- White wine
- Clear

WHEEL OF FLAVORS

Sweet
Honey
Fruity
Nutty
Floral
Malty
Body
Spicy
Smoky
Winey
Tobacco
Medicinal

OBSERVATIONS

WHISKEY

Distiller _____ Date _____

Origin _____ Strength _____

Location _____ Price _____

TASTE

Delicate ├──┼──┼──┼──┼──┼──┼──┤ Smoky

Light ├──┼──┼──┼──┼──┼──┼──┤ Rich

GLANCE

Oily

Watery

COLOR

Dark oak

Mahogany

Copper

Amber

Gold

Honey

Straw

White wine

Clear

WHEEL OF FLAVORS

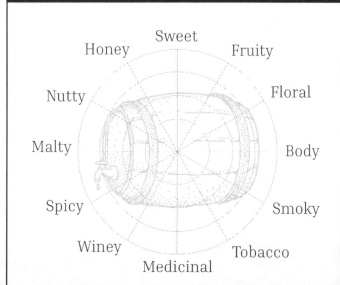

Sweet
Honey   Fruity
Nutty   Floral
Malty   Body
Spicy   Smoky
Winey   Tobacco
Medicinal

OBSERVATIONS

WHISKEY

Distiller

Origin

Location

Date

Strength

Price

TASTE

Delicate ├──┼──┼──┼──┼──┼──┼──┤ Smoky

Light ├──┼──┼──┼──┼──┼──┼──┤ Rich

GLANCE

Oily

Watery

COLOR

Dark oak

Mahogany

Copper

Amber

Gold

Honey

Straw

White wine

Clear

WHEEL OF FLAVORS

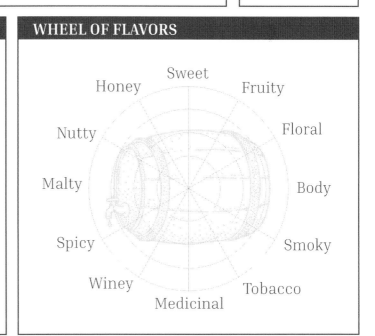

Sweet

Honey

Fruity

Nutty

Floral

Malty

Body

Spicy

Smoky

Winey

Tobacco

Medicinal

OBSERVATIONS

WHISKEY

Distiller _____ Date _____

Origin _____ Strength _____

Location _____ Price _____

TASTE

Delicate ├─┼─┼─┼─┼─┼─┼─┼─┤ Smoky

Light ├─┼─┼─┼─┼─┼─┼─┼─┤ Rich

GLANCE

Oily

Watery

COLOR

Dark oak

Mahogany

Copper

Amber

Gold

Honey

Straw

White wine

Clear

WHEEL OF FLAVORS

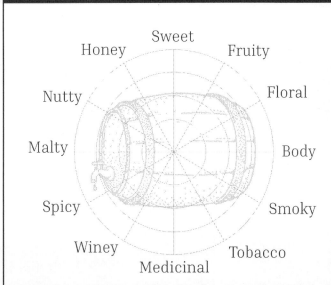

Sweet

Honey   Fruity

Nutty   Floral

Malty   Body

Spicy   Smoky

Winey   Tobacco

Medicinal

OBSERVATIONS

_____

_____

_____

_____

WHISKEY

RATING

Distiller

Date

Origin

Strength

Location

Price

TASTE

Delicate |———|———|———|———|———|———| Smoky

Light |———|———|———|———|———|———| Rich

GLANCE

Oily

Watery

COLOR

Dark oak

Mahogany

Copper

Amber

Gold

Honey

Straw

White wine

Clear

WHEEL OF FLAVORS

Sweet

Honey

Fruity

Nutty

Floral

Malty

Body

Spicy

Smoky

Winey

Tobacco

Medicinal

OBSERVATIONS

WHISKEY

Distiller   Date

Origin   Strength

Location   Price

TASTE

Delicate ├──┼──┼──┼──┼──┼──┼──┤ Smoky

Light ├──┼──┼──┼──┼──┼──┼──┤ Rich

GLANCE

Oily

Watery

COLOR

Dark oak

Mahogany

Copper

Amber

Gold

Honey

Straw

White wine

Clear

WHEEL OF FLAVORS

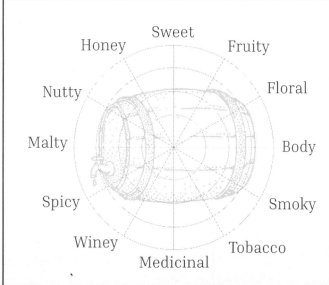

Sweet

Honey   Fruity

Nutty   Floral

Malty   Body

Spicy   Smoky

Winey   Tobacco

Medicinal

OBSERVATIONS

WHISKEY

Distiller   Date

Origin   Strength

Location   Price

TASTE

Delicate ├──┼──┼──┼──┼──┼──┤ Smoky

Light ├──┼──┼──┼──┼──┼──┤ Rich

GLANCE

Oily

Watery

COLOR

Dark oak

Mahogany

Copper

Amber

Gold

Honey

Straw

White wine

Clear

WHEEL OF FLAVORS

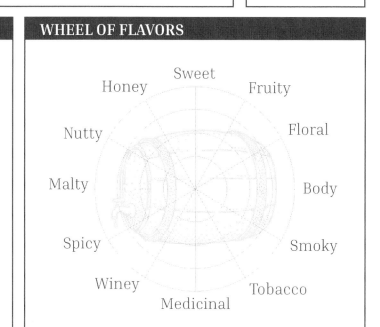

Sweet

Honey   Fruity

Nutty   Floral

Malty   Body

Spicy   Smoky

Winey   Tobacco

Medicinal

OBSERVATIONS

WHISKEY

Distiller _____   Date _____

Origin _____   Strength _____

Location _____   Price _____

TASTE

Delicate ├──┼──┼──┼──┼──┼──┼──┤ Smoky

Light ├──┼──┼──┼──┼──┼──┼──┤ Rich

GLANCE

Oily

Watery

COLOR

Dark oak

Mahogany

Copper

Amber

Gold

Honey

Straw

White wine

Clear

WHEEL OF FLAVORS

Sweet

Honey   Fruity

Nutty   Floral

Malty   Body

Spicy   Smoky

Winey   Tobacco

Medicinal

OBSERVATIONS

WHISKEY

RATING

Distiller	Date
Origin	Strength
Location	Price

TASTE

Delicate ├──┼──┼──┼──┼──┼──┼──┤ Smoky

Light ├──┼──┼──┼──┼──┼──┼──┤ Rich

GLANCE

Oily

Watery

COLOR

Dark oak

Mahogany

Copper

Amber

Gold

Honey

Straw

White wine

Clear

WHEEL OF FLAVORS

Sweet

Honey

Fruity

Nutty

Floral

Malty

Body

Spicy

Smoky

Winey

Tobacco

Medicinal

OBSERVATIONS

71

WHISKEY

Distiller

Origin

Location

Date

Strength

Price

TASTE

Delicate ├─────────────┤ Smoky

Light ├─────────────┤ Rich

GLANCE

Oily

Watery

COLOR

Dark oak

Mahogany

Copper

Amber

Gold

Honey

Straw

White wine

Clear

WHEEL OF FLAVORS

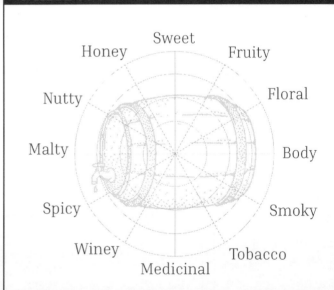

Sweet

Honey   Fruity

Nutty   Floral

Malty   Body

Spicy   Smoky

Winey   Tobacco

Medicinal

OBSERVATIONS

WHISKEY

RATING

Distiller

Origin

Location

Date

Strength

Price

TASTE

Delicate ├──┼──┼──┼──┼──┼──┼──┤ Smoky

Light ├──┼──┼──┼──┼──┼──┼──┤ Rich

GLANCE

Oily

Watery

COLOR

Dark oak

Mahogany

Copper

Amber

Gold

Honey

Straw

White wine

Clear

WHEEL OF FLAVORS

Sweet

Honey

Fruity

Nutty

Floral

Malty

Body

Spicy

Smoky

Winey

Tobacco

Medicinal

OBSERVATIONS

WHISKEY

Distiller _____ 　 Date _____

Origin _____ 　 Strength _____

Location _____ 　 Price _____

TASTE

Delicate ├──┼──┼──┼──┼──┼──┤ Smoky

Light ├──┼──┼──┼──┼──┼──┤ Rich

GLANCE

Oily

Watery

COLOR

- Dark oak
- Mahogany
- Copper
- Amber
- Gold
- Honey
- Straw
- White wine
- Clear

WHEEL OF FLAVORS

Sweet
Honey
Fruity
Nutty
Floral
Malty
Body
Spicy
Smoky
Winey
Tobacco
Medicinal

OBSERVATIONS

_____

_____

_____

_____

WHISKEY

RATING

Distiller   Date

Origin   Strength

Location   Price

TASTE

Delicate ├──┼──┼──┼──┼──┼──┼──┤ Smoky

Light ├──┼──┼──┼──┼──┼──┼──┤ Rich

GLANCE

Oily

Watery

COLOR

Dark oak

Mahogany

Copper

Amber

Gold

Honey

Straw

White wine

Clear

WHEEL OF FLAVORS

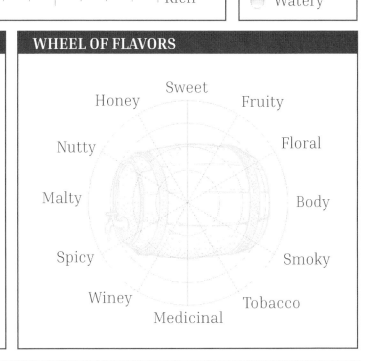

Sweet

Honey

Fruity

Nutty

Floral

Malty

Body

Spicy

Smoky

Winey

Tobacco

Medicinal

OBSERVATIONS

WHISKEY

RATING

Distiller

Origin

Location

Date

Strength

Price

TASTE

Delicate ├──┼──┼──┼──┼──┼──┼──┤ Smoky

Light ├──┼──┼──┼──┼──┼──┼──┤ Rich

GLANCE

Oily

Watery

COLOR

Dark oak

Mahogany

Copper

Amber

Gold

Honey

Straw

White wine

Clear

WHEEL OF FLAVORS

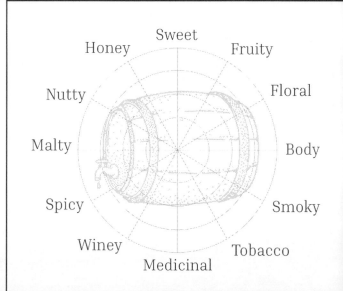

Sweet

Honey

Fruity

Nutty

Floral

Malty

Body

Spicy

Smoky

Winey

Tobacco

Medicinal

OBSERVATIONS

WHISKEY

Distiller

Origin

Location

Date

Strength

Price

TASTE

Delicate ├──┼──┼──┼──┼──┼──┼──┤ Smoky

Light ├──┼──┼──┼──┼──┼──┼──┤ Rich

GLANCE

Oily

Watery

COLOR

Dark oak

Mahogany

Copper

Amber

Gold

Honey

Straw

White wine

Clear

WHEEL OF FLAVORS

Sweet

Honey   Fruity

Nutty   Floral

Malty   Body

Spicy   Smoky

Winey   Tobacco

Medicinal

OBSERVATIONS

WHISKEY

Distiller _____

Origin _____

Location _____

Date _____

Strength _____

Price _____

TASTE

Delicate ├──┼──┼──┼──┼──┼──┤ Smoky

Light ├──┼──┼──┼──┼──┼──┤ Rich

GLANCE

Oily

Watery

COLOR

- Dark oak
- Mahogany
- Copper
- Amber
- Gold
- Honey
- Straw
- White wine
- Clear

WHEEL OF FLAVORS

Sweet

Honey   Fruity

Nutty   Floral

Malty   Body

Spicy   Smoky

Winey   Tobacco

Medicinal

OBSERVATIONS

WHISKEY

Distiller   Date

Origin   Strength

Location   Price

TASTE

Delicate ├──┼──┼──┼──┼──┼──┼──┤ Smoky

Light ├──┼──┼──┼──┼──┼──┼──┤ Rich

GLANCE

Oily

Watery

COLOR

Dark oak

Mahogany

Copper

Amber

Gold

Honey

Straw

White wine

Clear

WHEEL OF FLAVORS

Sweet

Honey

Fruity

Nutty

Floral

Malty

Body

Spicy

Smoky

Winey

Tobacco

Medicinal

OBSERVATIONS

WHISKEY

RATING

Distiller ....

Origin ....

Location ....

Date ....

Strength ....

Price ....

TASTE

Delicate ├──┼──┼──┼──┼──┼──┼──┤ Smoky

Light ├──┼──┼──┼──┼──┼──┼──┤ Rich

GLANCE

Oily

Watery

COLOR

Dark oak
Mahogany
Copper
Amber
Gold
Honey
Straw
White wine
Clear

WHEEL OF FLAVORS

Sweet
Honey
Fruity
Nutty
Floral
Malty
Body
Spicy
Smoky
Winey
Tobacco
Medicinal

OBSERVATIONS

WHISKEY

Distiller

Origin

Location

Date

Strength

Price

TASTE

Delicate |———|———|———|———|———|———| Smoky

Light |———|———|———|———|———|———| Rich

GLANCE

Oily

Watery

COLOR

Dark oak

Mahogany

Copper

Amber

Gold

Honey

Straw

White wine

Clear

WHEEL OF FLAVORS

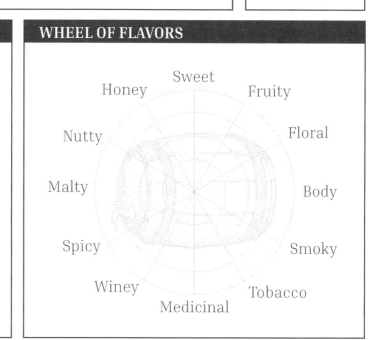

Sweet

Honey

Fruity

Nutty

Floral

Malty

Body

Spicy

Smoky

Winey

Tobacco

Medicinal

OBSERVATIONS

WHISKEY

RATING

Distiller _____   Date _____

Origin _____   Strength _____

Location _____   Price _____

TASTE

Delicate ├──┼──┼──┼──┼──┼──┼──┤ Smoky

Light ├──┼──┼──┼──┼──┼──┼──┤ Rich

GLANCE

Oily

Watery

COLOR

Dark oak

Mahogany

Copper

Amber

Gold

Honey

Straw

White wine

Clear

WHEEL OF FLAVORS

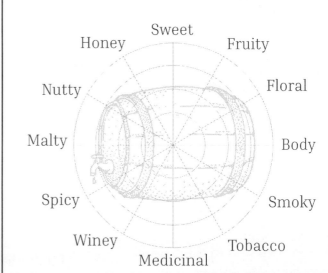

Sweet

Honey

Fruity

Nutty

Floral

Malty

Body

Spicy

Smoky

Winey

Tobacco

Medicinal

OBSERVATIONS

WHISKEY

RATING

Distiller

Date

Origin

Strength

Location

Price

TASTE

Delicate ├──┼──┼──┼──┼──┼──┼──┤ Smoky

Light ├──┼──┼──┼──┼──┼──┼──┤ Rich

GLANCE

Oily

Watery

COLOR

Dark oak

Mahogany

Copper

Amber

Gold

Honey

Straw

White wine

Clear

WHEEL OF FLAVORS

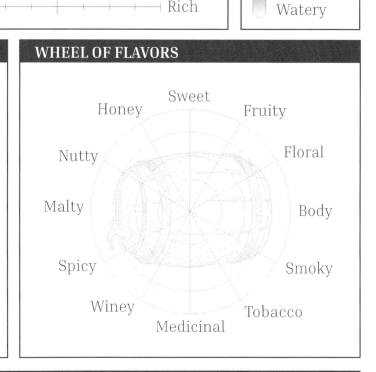

Sweet

Honey

Fruity

Nutty

Floral

Malty

Body

Spicy

Smoky

Winey

Tobacco

Medicinal

OBSERVATIONS

WHISKEY

Distiller _____   Date _____

Origin _____   Strength _____

Location _____   Price _____

TASTE

Delicate ├──┼──┼──┼──┼──┼──┼──┤ Smoky

Light ├──┼──┼──┼──┼──┼──┼──┤ Rich

GLANCE

 Oily

Watery

COLOR

- Dark oak
- Mahogany
- Copper
- Amber
- Gold
- Honey
- Straw
- White wine
- Clear

WHEEL OF FLAVORS

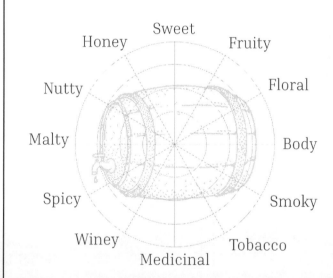

Sweet

Honey   Fruity

Nutty   Floral

Malty   Body

Spicy   Smoky

Winey   Tobacco

Medicinal

OBSERVATIONS

WHISKEY

RATING

Distiller

Origin

Location

Date

Strength

Price

TASTE

Delicate |—+—+—+—|—+—+—| Smoky

Light |—+—+—|—+—+—+—| Rich

GLANCE

Oily

Watery

COLOR

Dark oak

Mahogany

Copper

Amber

Gold

Honey

Straw

White wine

Clear

WHEEL OF FLAVORS

Sweet

Honey

Fruity

Nutty

Floral

Malty

Body

Spicy

Smoky

Winey

Tobacco

Medicinal

OBSERVATIONS

WHISKEY

Distiller _____   Date _____

Origin _____   Strength _____

Location _____   Price _____

TASTE

Delicate ├──┼──┼──┼──┼──┼──┼──┤ Smoky

Light ├──┼──┼──┼──┼──┼──┼──┤ Rich

GLANCE

Oily

Watery

COLOR

Dark oak

Mahogany

Copper

Amber

Gold

Honey

Straw

White wine

Clear

WHEEL OF FLAVORS

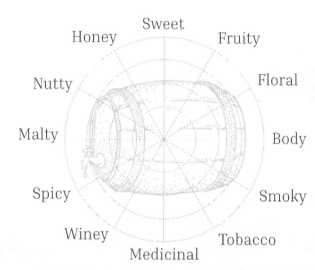

Sweet

Honey

Fruity

Nutty

Floral

Malty

Body

Spicy

Smoky

Winey

Tobacco

Medicinal

OBSERVATIONS

WHISKEY

RATING

Distiller

Date

Origin

Strength

Location

Price

TASTE

Delicate |—————————————| Smoky

Light |—————————————| Rich

GLANCE

Oily

Watery

COLOR

Dark oak

Mahogany

Copper

Amber

Gold

Honey

Straw

White wine

Clear

WHEEL OF FLAVORS

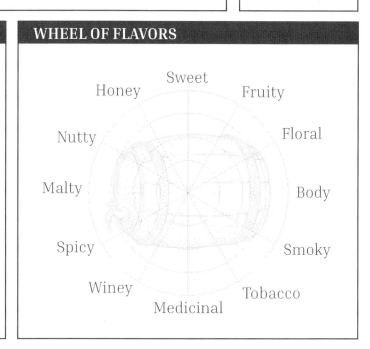

Sweet

Honey

Fruity

Nutty

Floral

Malty

Body

Spicy

Smoky

Winey

Tobacco

Medicinal

OBSERVATIONS

WHISKEY

Distiller ....

Origin ....

Location ....

Date ....

Strength ....

Price ....

TASTE

Delicate |—+—+—+—|—+—+—+—| Smoky

Light |—+—+—+—|—+—+—+—| Rich

GLANCE

Oily

Watery

COLOR

Dark oak

Mahogany

Copper

Amber

Gold

Honey

Straw

White wine

Clear

WHEEL OF FLAVORS

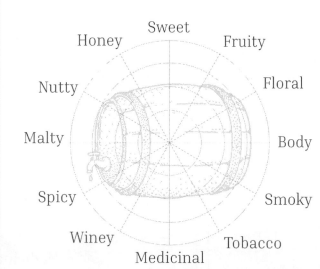

Sweet

Honey   Fruity

Nutty   Floral

Malty   Body

Spicy   Smoky

Winey   Tobacco

Medicinal

OBSERVATIONS

WHISKEY

Distiller

Origin

Location

Date

Strength

Price

TASTE

Delicate ├──┼──┼──┼──┼──┼──┤ Smoky

Light ├──┼──┼──┼──┼──┼──┤ Rich

GLANCE

Oily

Watery

COLOR

Dark oak

Mahogany

Copper

Amber

Gold

Honey

Straw

White wine

Clear

WHEEL OF FLAVORS

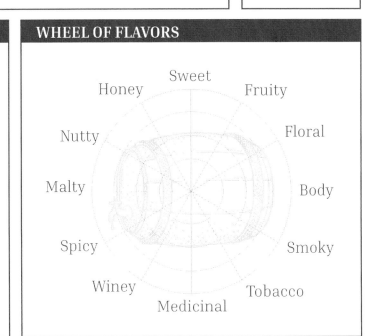

Sweet

Honey

Fruity

Nutty

Floral

Malty

Body

Spicy

Smoky

Winey

Tobacco

Medicinal

OBSERVATIONS

89

WHISKEY

RATING

Distiller ....   Date ....

Origin ....   Strength ....

Location ....   Price ....

TASTE

Delicate |——+——+——+——+——+——+——| Smoky

Light |——+——+——+——+——+——+——| Rich

GLANCE

Oily

Watery

COLOR

Dark oak

Mahogany

Copper

Amber

Gold

Honey

Straw

White wine

Clear

WHEEL OF FLAVORS

Sweet

Honey   Fruity

Nutty   Floral

Malty   Body

Spicy   Smoky

Winey   Tobacco

Medicinal

OBSERVATIONS

WHISKEY

RATING

Distiller

Origin

Location

Date

Strength

Price

TASTE

Delicate |——+——+——+——|——+——+——+——| Smoky

Light |——+——+——+——|——+——+——+——| Rich

GLANCE

Oily

Watery

COLOR

Dark oak

Mahogany

Copper

Amber

Gold

Honey

Straw

White wine

Clear

WHEEL OF FLAVORS

Sweet

Honey

Fruity

Nutty

Floral

Malty

Body

Spicy

Smoky

Winey

Tobacco

Medicinal

OBSERVATIONS

WHISKEY

Distiller _____ Date _____

Origin _____ Strength _____

Location _____ Price _____

TASTE

Delicate ├──┼──┼──┼──┼──┼──┼──┤ Smoky

Light ├──┼──┼──┼──┼──┼──┼──┤ Rich

GLANCE

Oily

Watery

COLOR

Dark oak

Mahogany

Copper

Amber

Gold

Honey

Straw

White wine

Clear

WHEEL OF FLAVORS

Sweet

Honey   Fruity

Nutty   Floral

Malty   Body

Spicy   Smoky

Winey   Tobacco

Medicinal

OBSERVATIONS

_____

_____

_____

_____

WHISKEY

Distiller   Date

Origin   Strength

Location   Price

TASTE

Delicate ├──┼──┼──┼──┼──┼──┼──┤ Smoky

Light ├──┼──┼──┼──┼──┼──┼──┤ Rich

GLANCE

Oily

Watery

COLOR

Dark oak

Mahogany

Copper

Amber

Gold

Honey

Straw

White wine

Clear

WHEEL OF FLAVORS

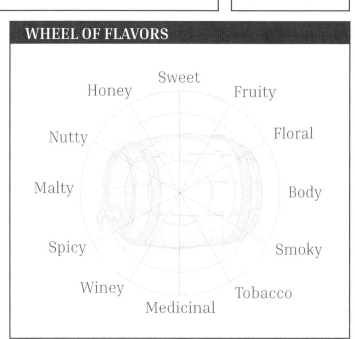

Sweet

Honey   Fruity

Nutty   Floral

Malty   Body

Spicy   Smoky

Winey   Tobacco

Medicinal

OBSERVATIONS

WHISKEY

RATING

Distiller ....
Origin ....
Location ....

Date ....
Strength ....
Price ....

TASTE

Delicate ├──┼──┼──┼──┼──┼──┼──┤ Smoky

Light ├──┼──┼──┼──┼──┼──┼──┤ Rich

GLANCE

Oily

Watery

COLOR

Dark oak
Mahogany
Copper
Amber
Gold
Honey
Straw
White wine
Clear

WHEEL OF FLAVORS

Sweet
Honey   Fruity
Nutty
                    Floral
Malty
                    Body
Spicy
                    Smoky
Winey
        Medicinal Tobacco

OBSERVATIONS

....
....
....
....

WHISKEY

Distiller   Date

Origin   Strength

Location   Price

TASTE

Delicate ├─────────────────────┤ Smoky

Light ├─────────────────────┤ Rich

GLANCE

Oily

Watery

COLOR

Dark oak

Mahogany

Copper

Amber

Gold

Honey

Straw

White wine

Clear

WHEEL OF FLAVORS

Sweet

Honey   Fruity

Nutty   Floral

Malty   Body

Spicy   Smoky

Winey   Tobacco

Medicinal

OBSERVATIONS

WHISKEY

Distiller ....   Date ....

Origin ....   Strength ....

Location ....   Price ....

TASTE

Delicate ├────┼────┼────┼────┤ Smoky

Light ├────┼────┼────┼────┤ Rich

GLANCE

Oily

Watery

COLOR

Dark oak
Mahogany
Copper
Amber
Gold
Honey
Straw
White wine
Clear

WHEEL OF FLAVORS

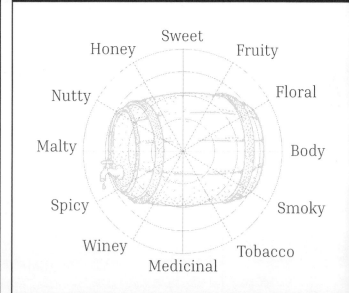

Sweet

Honey   Fruity

Nutty   Floral

Malty   Body

Spicy   Smoky

Winey   Tobacco

Medicinal

OBSERVATIONS

WHISKEY

RATING

Distiller

Date

Origin

Strength

Location

Price

TASTE

Delicate ├─────┼─────┼─────┼─────┼─────┤ Smoky

Light ├─────┼─────┼─────┼─────┼─────┤ Rich

GLANCE

Oily

Watery

COLOR

Dark oak

Mahogany

Copper

Amber

Gold

Honey

Straw

White wine

Clear

WHEEL OF FLAVORS

Sweet

Honey

Fruity

Nutty

Floral

Malty

Body

Spicy

Smoky

Winey

Tobacco

Medicinal

OBSERVATIONS

WHISKEY

Distiller ....

Origin ....

Location ....

Date ....

Strength ....

Price ....

TASTE

Delicate ├──┼──┼──┼──┼──┼──┼──┤ Smoky

Light ├──┼──┼──┼──┼──┼──┼──┤ Rich

GLANCE

Oily

Watery

COLOR

Dark oak

Mahogany

Copper

Amber

Gold

Honey

Straw

White wine

Clear

WHEEL OF FLAVORS

Sweet

Honey

Fruity

Nutty

Floral

Malty

Body

Spicy

Smoky

Winey

Tobacco

Medicinal

OBSERVATIONS

WHISKEY

RATING

Distiller

Origin

Location

Date

Strength

Price

TASTE

Delicate |————————————| Smoky

Light |————————————| Rich

GLANCE

Oily

Watery

COLOR

Dark oak
Mahogany
Copper
Amber
Gold
Honey
Straw
White wine
Clear

WHEEL OF FLAVORS

Sweet
Honey   Fruity
Nutty   Floral
Malty   Body
Spicy   Smoky
Winey   Tobacco
Medicinal

OBSERVATIONS

WHISKEY

Distiller .... Date ....

Origin .... Strength ....

Location .... Price ....

TASTE

Delicate ├──┼──┼──┼──┼──┼──┼──┤ Smoky

Light ├──┼──┼──┼──┼──┼──┼──┤ Rich

GLANCE

Oily

Watery

COLOR

- Dark oak
- Mahogany
- Copper
- Amber
- Gold
- Honey
- Straw
- White wine
- Clear

WHEEL OF FLAVORS

Sweet

Honey   Fruity

Nutty   Floral

Malty   Body

Spicy   Smoky

Winey   Tobacco

Medicinal

OBSERVATIONS

WHISKEY

RATING

Distiller   Date

Origin   Strength

Location   Price

TASTE

Delicate |—+—+—+—+—+—+—+—| Smoky

Light |—+—+—+—+—+—+—+—| Rich

GLANCE

Oily

Watery

COLOR

Dark oak

Mahogany

Copper

Amber

Gold

Honey

Straw

White wine

Clear

WHEEL OF FLAVORS

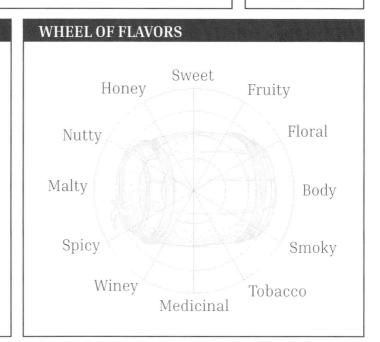

Sweet

Honey   Fruity

Nutty   Floral

Malty   Body

Spicy   Smoky

Winey   Tobacco

Medicinal

OBSERVATIONS

WHISKEY

Distiller _____   Date _____

Origin _____   Strength _____

Location _____   Price _____

TASTE

Delicate ├──┼──┼──┼──┼──┼──┼──┤ Smoky

Light ├──┼──┼──┼──┼──┼──┼──┤ Rich

GLANCE

Oily

Watery

COLOR

- Dark oak
- Mahogany
- Copper
- Amber
- Gold
- Honey
- Straw
- White wine
- Clear

WHEEL OF FLAVORS

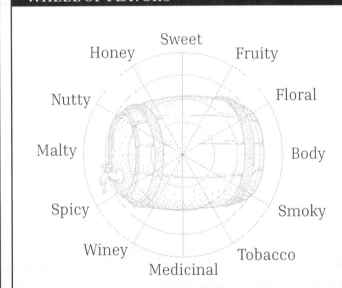

Sweet

Honey   Fruity

Nutty   Floral

Malty   Body

Spicy   Smoky

Winey   Tobacco

Medicinal

OBSERVATIONS

_____

_____

_____

_____

WHISKEY

	RATING

Distiller   Date

Origin   Strength

Location   Price

TASTE

Delicate ├──┼──┼──┼──┼──┼──┼──┤ Smoky

Light ├──┼──┼──┼──┼──┼──┼──┤ Rich

GLANCE

Oily

Watery

COLOR

Dark oak

Mahogany

Copper

Amber

Gold

Honey

Straw

White wine

Clear

WHEEL OF FLAVORS

Sweet

Honey   Fruity

Nutty   Floral

Malty   Body

Spicy   Smoky

Winey   Tobacco

Medicinal

OBSERVATIONS

Made in the USA
Coppell, TX
01 May 2023

16289265R00062